T0150458

WHAT IS A NONGRADED PRIMARY?

What is the most effective way to educate young children? Whether or not the nongraded primary is the answer, this publication is meant to stimulate discussion on this vital topic among educators, parents, and the community. *The Nongraded Primary...Making Schools Fit Children* explains the concept of nongraded primary education and provides insights from education leaders, along with examples of successful programs.

The concept of a nongraded primary is not new. In practice, it is an umbrella term and its names are as varied as the school districts that have tried it: multiage grouping, multi-age classes, mixed-age grouping, ungraded primary, family grouping, heterogeneous grouping, vertical grouping, and primary school nongraded.

THE NONGRADED MOVEMENT

Nongraded classrooms, researchers point out, date back to the "one-room school" that was the norm up until the 19th century or much later in some communities, where children of different ages learned together.

PROGRESS AT AN INDIVIDUAL RATE.

In simplest terms, the nongraded schools model allows pupils to advance from one concept/skill level to the next as they are ready, regardless of age or grade. Such a plan embraces the kindergarten program plus what are normally the first three grades of the elementary school.

Those unfamiliar with the term "nongraded" often think it refers to the practice of not giving letter grades. Author Joan Gaustad, in her article "Making the Transition from Graded to Nongraded Primary Education," explains that a nongraded primary is much broader than this assumption. She defines nongraded education as the "practice of teaching children of different ages and ability levels together, without dividing the curriculum into steps labeled by grade designations."

Rather than passing or failing at the end of the year, children progress through the curriculum at their own individual rates. The use of letter grades is often replaced by different types of assessment, such as collections of student work, demonstrations, and descriptive reports.

A TIMELY IDEA.

Regardless of its name, the nongraded primary has become a key element in educational reforms being enacted across the nation. As state education policymakers begin to rely less on standardized tests and to address the fact that children learn at different rates, the issue of nongraded classrooms is being revisited, says Chris Pipho of the Education Commission of the States.

John I. Goodlad and Robert H. Anderson, authors of the book, *The Nongraded Elementary School,* cite 1970s research showing that standardized achievement test comparisons "tend to favor" nongraded programs, and that students in those programs may have improved chances of good mental health and positive school attitudes. They suggest the nongraded model is "particularly beneficial" for minorities, boys, underachievers, and low-income pupils.

ABOLISH TRADITIONAL GRADES, SAY ELEMENTARY PRINCIPALS

Traditional grade levels in the first five years of school should be abolished, said a 1990 survey of elementary school principals.

Two-thirds of principals believe abolishing traditional grade levels would be advantageous to restructuring elementary education, said the survey by the National Association of Elementary School Principals.

The survey also found that the principals believe all-day kindergarten, smaller classes, and a longer academic year are among the ways principals could restructure services in the first five years of school.

One-third of the principals surveyed said they would rather expand the curriculum to help children develop emotional and social skills. Principals also would like to give teachers flexibility to organize their school day and set aside more time for outside tutoring, the survey said.

Source: *Education USA*, April 16, 1990

THE BOTTOM LINE FOR CHILDREN

The major belief behind the nongraded primary is that it can improve the teaching and learning environment for students to enhance student achievement. In short, mounting evidence shows that the nongraded primary can have the following benefits:

- An opportunity for children to succeed rather than fail;
- Enhanced cooperation and reduced conflict among staff, parents, and schools; and
- Increased levels of community support and confidence in the schools.

In the words of Linda Hargan of the Kentucky Department of Education:

"I really think the nongraded primary school is going to let us put in place a lot of things we already know are the best things for children, but that the system has precluded us from being able to implement effectively...It is really a vote of confidence for the children. It says that children can learn if we give them the opportunity and appropriate instruction and an environment in which they feel good about themselves—they will learn and they will thrive."

AVOIDING FAILURE.

David Hornbeck, one of the developers of the Kentucky Education Reform Act, which established a nongraded program statewide, believes educators are finally realizing the current, rigid structure of most schools has added to situations where children are labeled as "failures" because they have not achieved a certain standard at a certain time.

"One of the reasons I recommended it [a nongraded primary] in Kentucky," Hornbeck says, "is that there's a lot of evidence that for kids to fail in kindergarten or first grade has devastating consequences to it. That hooks back to the developmental issue—if you don't have a first grade, you can't fail it!"

In Kentucky, prekindergarten through third grade "was wiped out" in the education reform plan. "Frankly, there was no particular reason that it needs to stop at third grade. My reason? I didn't want to overdo it," Hornbeck says. " Secondly, the developmental variation is greater in the younger years."

THE TESTING CONTROVERSY.

Hornbeck says when previous nongraded primary efforts were taking place in the 1960s, the emphasis on outcomes "was about nonexistent." So, he adds, there were no real goals or accountability. Schools, he says, must establish outcomes and have good assessment instruments—which to Hornbeck does not mean standardized tests.

Like many education groups today, Hornbeck believes standardized tests have no positive, direct usefulness in guiding instruction, and that their indirect influence—implicitly laying down goals and standards—disrupts or blocks teaching.

"The key is establishing those standards," Hornbeck says. "To use Kentucky as an example, we established the points of accountability at the fourth-grade level—what kids ought to know and be able to do at the fourth grade. That established the standard at which teachers can determine what kids ought to know and be able to do at an age between eight and 10 and move on."

CONCERNS ABOUT THE NONGRADED PRIMARY

Although the concept of nongraded primary education is gaining momentum across the country, many educators and parents still have important questions about the movement. Here are some of their most common concerns:

- Instruction in the nongraded primary is a dramatic departure from the status quo, which some educators may find threatening. Teachers who are not trained to work with different ages at once initially may resist the nongraded movement.

- Discipline in a nongraded classroom is a potential problem, despite the theory that mixed-age grouping fosters good discipline because older children take on roles as leaders and models for the younger ones.

- America's textbook publishing system serves mainly single-grade classrooms and impedes the transition to nongraded education. In the "scope and sequence" models of the last decade, children at every grade level trained in carefully delineated subject areas before they moved on to the next grade.

- Combining older and younger children in the same classes will make older children appear "slow." Also, teachers of mixed-age groups sometimes provide fewer challenges for older children. On the other hand, a perceived gap between the work of older and younger children may frustrate younger students.

In 1986, Ernest L. Boyer, president of the Carnegie Foundation for the Advancement of Teaching and one of the nation's most respected education leaders, first proposed the concept of the Basic School—a nongraded program for children through the fourth grade.

The Basic School, he suggested, would focus on teaching some basic skills (language and computing), have no rigid grade levels, encourage individual instruction, and limit class size to 15 students per teacher.

In an interview, Boyer discussed the resurgence of interest in the nongraded primary program today and the apparent mistrust by some teachers of the whole idea of mixed-age grouping in early childhood classrooms.

"It has been my observation that educators seem to exhaust themselves over issues such as phonics versus nonphonics, nongraded versus graded, and so forth," Boyer says. "Why we seem always to organize our 'crusades' around these ideologies of 'good' and 'bad' is not clear. What's really at stake here, in my opinion, is the larger question of what are the best ways to group students to make their learning most effective? In other words, grouping that fits the education program."

Boyer doesn't deny that, at times, students may be grouped by age for administrative purposes, such as recordkeeping. "Let's get on with that," he says, "but once organized, to say that's the only way students can learn is simply nonsense."

"Children should not be kept chronologically frozen," Boyer says. He decries the increasing segregation of society today into age groups. "There are three-year-olds in day-care centers, five-year-olds in kindergarten, college students isolated and alone, older people in retirement villages.

"Children are locked in a prison of their own birthday and are not allowed the richness they deserve. To have first and fourth graders working together in certain projects benefits both. Older children need to teach younger children. Younger children can be inspired by older ones. I think there is great advantage in grouping children for learning that cuts across age and ethnicities and abilities."

Boyer sees parents as active partners and supporters of the nongraded classroom if educators are willing to offer them a rational explanation and "not a new religion we are going to start to worship."

"The school, teachers, and parents have to understand that we are going to be grouping children in different ways," he says. "Parents will understand that this makes sense. They understand how at home it is to the family's advantage to work together on some projects. Some goals can be accomplished more effectively than others. Their support will be established by the power of our arguments and the persuasion of our convictions. The classroom should be a staging ground for action."

And what does the nongraded primary mean for teachers? "I would think they would be joyful and enthusiastic," Boyer says. "It adds richness and empowerment for teachers. Rather than a threat, it's an opportunity for freedom."

Boyer said teachers will be able to involve students of different ages and work collaboratively with other teachers "rather than having the burden of staying in the same classroom all day and working alone." The way some schools are structured today, there is no way for teachers to do anything but meet with the kids in the classroom, Boyer says. Teachers must be allowed time not only to do their own class preparation, but to work with colleagues on the school's vision. In the nongraded setting, teachers will come to be less isolated and team up with other teachers to share ideas and resources about the most developmentally appropriate methods.

"ALTHOUGH HUMANS ARE NOT USUALLY BORN IN LITTERS, WE SEEM TO INSIST THAT THEY BE EDUCATED IN THEM."

—THE CASE FOR MIXED-AGE GROUPING IN EARLY EDUCATION,
LILIAN G. KATZ, DEMETRA EVANGELOU, AND JEANETTE ALLISON HARTMAN

BELIEFS ABOUT THE NONGRADED PRIMARY

The nongraded movement is not associated with any particular type of school system. Instead, school, district, and state initiatives across the country share a number of common beliefs:

○ The nongraded primary frees children from an arbitrary timeframe. Children grow and develop at different rates in their early years. In the nongraded primary, teachers do not arbitrarily make a determination about whether students are ahead or behind when they are five, six, or seven years old.

○ Children can work with other children who are at various levels. In doing so, they learn a great deal through social interaction. The classroom becomes a laboratory for learning. Whether the child is the brightest or slowest, he or she can operate at his or her own level in a group.

○ Teachers change from being a transmitter of knowledge to a more active role of supporter, guide, and facilitator of children's learning. Teachers can see the natural strengths of a child and develop those strengths, rather than seeing the child as something to be "fixed."

○ Teachers are able to work together to make sure that learning takes place. Children can have the same teacher or teaching team for more than one year. This approach allows teachers to use what they have learned about a child in the first year for planning learning experiences the next year.

○ Parent-teacher communication is enhanced. The nongraded primary recognizes the immediate and important relationship between parents and teachers in the education of an individual child and the quality of education the child receives.

○ The educational opportunity for all children, including those from poor and minority families, is improved. For example, many districts use readiness tests that dispropor-tionately identify minority and poor children as being "unready" for school. In the nongraded setting, schools do not exclude young children on the basis of tests—particularly poor children who have the most to gain from early educational opportunities.

TRADITIONAL PRIMARY CLASSROOM

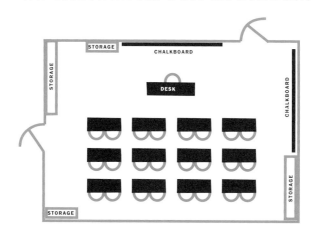

DEVELOPMENTAL PRIMARY CLASSROOM

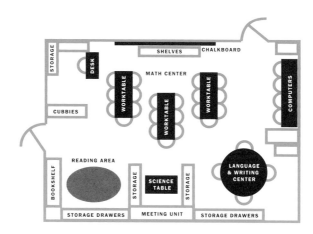

Adapted from: San Diego City Schools

CHARACTERISTICS OF THE NONGRADED PRIMARY

A nongraded primary *is*:

- ⇌ Developmentally appropriate curricula for primary age children.
- ⇌ A heterogeneous community of learners as related to age and ability.
- ⇌ Supportive of continuous learning.
- ⇌ Committed to honoring the development of the whole child.
- ⇌ Conducive to active student involvement—hands-on activities, classroom discussions and projects, concrete experiences related to real life examples, discovery, and student-initiated learning.
- ⇌ A teacher operating as the classroom facilitator—modeling, monitoring, observing, and giving guided instruction.
- ⇌ An emphasis on the process of learning.
- ⇌ A provider of an integrated curriculum across many subject areas so that children learn concepts and processes in a meaningful context.
- ⇌ Free of rigid instructional structures that impede learning, such as fixed ability grouping, grade levels, retention, and promotion.
- ⇌ Evaluated continuously using multiple data sources such as portfolios, anecdotal records, and samples of student work, as well as formal evaluation measures.

A nongraded primary *is not*:

- ⇌ An excuse for using the "back-to-basics" movement to narrow the curriculum and adopt instructional approaches that are incompatible with current knowledge about how young children learn and develop.
- ⇌ Based on rigid ability groups or age/grade groupings.
- ⇌ A static, lock-step learning system with little regard for a child's interest or motivation to move vertically (advancing upward into a higher grade level) and horizontally as he or she is interested in new knowledge.
- ⇌ An emphasis on learning based solely on the intellectual domain defined as discrete, technical, academic skills.
- ⇌ Work time where children are expected to work silently and alone on worksheets or with teacher-directed groups where a lecture or "Round Robin" reading in a circle occurs.
- ⇌ The teacher at the front of the room all day as the "sage on the stage."
- ⇌ An isolated learning of subjects with worksheets to support teaching and little relationship of concepts among subject areas, with the day divided into individual time segments for each subject area, and learning not seen as a part of the whole.
- ⇌ A system that considers grades are the motivator for children to do work.

Source: Nancy Barker, Vickey Herold, *Mixed-Age Class Information*, Carrollton-Farmers Branch Independent School District, Texas.

CHANGE IN THE NONGRADED PRIMARY

CHANGING ROLES

The move to any school-level model calls for everyone involved in the education enterprise to examine traditional roles and, in some cases, to adopt new roles. Although everyone will have a different contribution to make in a nongraded primary program, all efforts should be focused on the ultimate goal of improving education for young children.

Good planning suggests the importance of defining each person's role in the beginning. Positive change is more likely to occur when all the significant players align their efforts around a common agenda.

TEACHERS.

The nongraded organization implies that learning begins where the child is and moves forward as the child is able. This progress occurs in the classroom, where the teacher continuously adjusts the learning environment to meet the individual learning needs of each child. Teachers, therefore, are the foundation upon which a successful nongraded primary is built.

For many teachers, the transition to a nongraded program will require specialized training and additional study. Yet, these increased responsibilities will provide teachers with an opportunity to expand their professionalism. In a traditional school, teachers, parents, and the public relied on test scores and rigid criteria to pinpoint how well children, and thereby teachers, were doing. In the nongraded primary movement, on the other hand, teachers must work even harder to define what achievement and performance mean, both for themselves and for children.

PRINCIPALS.

The principal is central to school improvement. In the nongraded school setting, the principal is the education leader—a person who is truly accountable for what takes place in the school. He or she should have confidence in the staff and free them of unnecessary pressures so that they can carry out their responsibilities. The principal sets the tone for the school and approaches change enthusiastically.

However, the principal is careful not to threaten teachers' security, but to make them feel they are part of a larger school and community team dedicated to helping children learn. "Nongraded must be his or her [the principal's] way of life,'" writes Lee I. Smith in the book, *Teaching in a Nongraded School.*

CENTRAL OFFICE STAFF.

Central office staff also are important contributors to the nongraded effort. Their attitude and the quality of assistance they provide will have a great influence on the program's success.

Central staff members can work with teachers in staff training activities to help them develop the skills they will need to work in this new arena. For example, curriculum specialists could show teachers how to integrate subjects and teach multiple levels.

The central office staff can help develop a shared mission for the new program throughout the school system. They also play a part in building understanding through talks and visits in the community.

SUPERINTENDENTS.

Research on school improvement and organizational change suggests that it doesn't happen without strong leadership and support. The school district's chief executive officer—the superintendent—leads the way.

One of the first things the superintendent can do is involve central office staff in the transition to and implementation of a nongraded primary program. Research reports and other materials on developmentally appropriate education should be available to staff members. Teachers and administrators from other districts working with the nongraded primary can be brought in as resources. Educators also can gain firsthand experience by visiting other districts involved in nongraded education to observe and ask questions. Staff members that are informed and actively involved are more likely to support and help "sell" a nongraded program in their home district.

The superintendent also should meet with parents to discuss the potential benefits of nongraded education. A 1990-91 study of 10 established nongraded programs, cosponsored by the Kentucky Education Association and the Appalachia Educational Laboratory, found "lack of parent and teacher understanding of the nongraded primary concept" was most frequently reported as the biggest obstacle to overcome in establishing nongraded programs.

As the leader of a school system, a superintendent who is building support for a nongraded primary should "live, breathe, walk, and talk it." If the superintendent is excited about a nongraded primary and its potential for improving education, his or her enthusiasm will spread to others.

LOCAL BOARDS OF EDUCATION.

A key to the success of the nongraded primary is local board support. Without their endorsement, enthusiasm, patience, and willingness to allow schools to succeed, the initiative will not work. The school board's primary duties will be to agree on appropriate goals and policy, monitor progress, allocate resources, work collaboratively with the superintendent, and serve as a decision-maker of last resort.

Along with the superintendent, the school board supports efforts to inform the community about nongraded education. And most important, board members must provide the necessary financial support for teacher training, equipping classrooms, and other needs.

PARENTS.

Because the nongraded primary emphasizes the developmental process of their children, parents become even more active partners in the nongraded primary. In fact, parents will likely be asked to accept an even greater role in helping their students learn. How? Some will reinforce at home what their children are learning in school. Some will get directly involved in classroom activities. Others will do both.

While most parents are pressed for time, they still want to have a voice in their children's education. Their willingness to be part of the school's education team will help teachers become even more effective. When teachers and parents regularly share information, students get an even better education.

Lynn Goya, a parent at Jarabek Elementary in the San Diego City Schools served on a task force appointed after the board of education requested that work begin on a nongraded primary program leading to student success.

"Perhaps nothing is more essential to improving children's education than the increased awareness and participation of the family and the community," Goya says. "The schools cannot and should not try to be an atlas where the whole burden of raising the next generation falls on the educator's shoulders. We must reestablish children as a national priority by insisting on establishing the value a student places on education. Without the excitement of learning and the desire to excel, no student, no matter how bright or fortunate, will succeed.

"The issues, then, are how to get the family involved, at what level, and how to manage that involvement most effectively....Parents need to be involved at all levels, from volunteering in the classroom to working with the teacher to establishing goals and directions for their own children; to participating in the decision-making process at the schools and at the district level; to raising supplemental funds; to working within the political process to ensure education's fair share of resources."

SCHOOL AND COMMUNITY GROUPS.

Everyone can play a key role in nongraded education. School groups ranging from the PTA and other parent organizations to community and school committees can make contributions on behalf of young children.

Businesses might "adopt" schools in order to provide volunteers who serve as role models for children. Civic and religious organizations could set special dates and programs to focus on education or to provide services such as reading or tutoring students. Still other organizations could work with teachers in taking the classroom to the community by sponsoring field trips. In turn, all these activities can enhance student achievement.

PRINCIPLES TO CONSIDER IN PLANNING A NONGRADED PRIMARY PROGRAM

1. **A child learns as a total person.** Knowledge and skills must be learned through all areas...physical, social, emotional, and intellectual...to help children learn how to learn and to establish the foundation for continuous lifelong learning.

2. **Children grow through similar stages of development, but at different rates and in different styles.** Every child is unique. Different levels of development and understanding affect every learning task. Children must be allowed to move at their own pace in acquiring skills. Most will learn these in their own time by the age of seven or eight.

3. **The way children feel about themselves and their sense of competence in learning impacts every learning act.** The way a child receives information may be as important to learning as the information received. Methods, climate, atmosphere, and teacher attitude all affect the child's self-esteem.

4. **Children learn best in active ways through interaction with the environment and with people.** Teacher planning time is best spent preparing the environment for active learning. As children interact with each other, with teachers, and with a variety of materials, they apply all types of learning processes.

5. **Children learn best when they are taught through an integrated curriculum that allows for pattern-building and selection of a wide variety of sensory data.** Projects, learning centers, and real-life activities related to the interests of children promote learning of concepts and skills through application and meaningful practice.

6. **Children cannot be given knowledge.** They must construct it for themselves through continuous action in their environments. Knowledge is constructed as a pattern of mental representations. It can only be constructed through action on materials. Each child's construction of knowledge is personal and unique. No two children, therefore, come to know something in exactly the same ways. Playful activity is the natural method of learning for young children.

7. **Learning is a very social process.** As children converse with others about interesting projects and ideas, they expand their language and thinking. Through conversation about the happenings in their lives, children are encouraged to expand their abilities to communicate orally, as well as through reading and writing.

8. **Children learn the skills of communication and expression when they are given many opportunities to share their learning with others through a variety of forms.** In a good language and literacy program, children are encouraged to expand all their communication skills.

9. **Children learn math skills and processes when they are encouraged to explore, discover, and solve real mathematics problems through both spontaneous and planned activities.** The math program in an elementary school should be designed to interest children in thinking and organizing experiences in mathematical ways, rather than to teach rote computation.

10. **Children learn best when the classroom environment is organized but flexible, and when developmentally appropriate tasks are encouraged.** Disorganization, inappropriate expectations, and emphasis on paper-pencil activities can quickly lead to stress and related problems in young children.

Source: *Developing an Appropriate Learning Environment for Children Five through Eight Years Old,* Southern Association on Children Under Six.

VEHICLES FOR CHANGE

Successful nongraded primary programs, says education writer Joan Gaustad, share implementation and maintenance practices in many important areas, including:

- ⊃ Advance study and planning
- ⊃ Flexibility in implementation
- ⊃ Practical training for teachers
- ⊃ Ongoing planning time
- ⊃ Informed and educated teachers and parents.

ADVANCE STUDY AND PLANNING.

Teachers and parents need time to consider nongrading and become comfortable with it to help the program succeed. The process of moving to a nongraded program is not accomplished overnight.

Advance study and planning creates a time to share with colleagues at the school any materials, notes, readings, and impressions of the nongraded primary. Teachers and parents need time to consider nongrading and become comfortable with it. The nongraded system forces a complete reevaluation of what the school is trying to accomplish.

"It would be difficult to do it instantly," says Hornbeck of the Kentucky Department of Education. "People need to work on it, understand it, think on it, discuss it, see other people participating in it. I think, organized right, it ought to be warmly embraced by teachers."

FLEXIBILITY IN IMPLEMENTATION.

In moving to the nongraded primary, the key word is flexibility. As Gaustad notes, "Adding a few new elements at a time generally works better than attempting to change the entire structure at once. Each new element should be evaluated and adjusted as program participants see how it works in practice, in their own unique circumstances."

Susan Bredekamp of the National Association for the Education of Young Children believes, "It [a nongraded primary program] does need to be a step at a time. I think it shouldn't start necessarily with doing away with grades. It should start with looking at how we teach, how we assess, what our curriculum is, and what our expectations are…"

PRACTICAL TRAINING FOR TEACHERS.

Teachers need time to train and share ideas about the ways they assist children and approach their teaching. While some teaching skills are effective in both single-grade and nongraded classrooms, different skills also are required.

The Carrollton-Farmers Branch School District in Texas has provided teachers with training opportunities that are particularly supportive of a nongraded approach to education. Training areas include cooperative learning and reading and writing processes. In addition to these specific training programs, teachers begin meeting regularly in the summer. They use study materials consisting of research syntheses, journal articles, and excerpts from current professional publications on such topics as assessment/evaluation, parent-teacher relations, motivation, and teaching strategies.

ONGOING PLANNING TIME.

Experts agree that teaching in the nongraded primary requires more preparation time. This time should be part of the official schedule for teachers.

In *Teaching in a Nongraded School*, Smith adds, "Teachers should do some long-range planning so that they can organize their thinking in relation to the broad units of work which are to be considered. A teacher should consider any purposes that the children might have and plan a program that will stimulate their interests and challenge their abilities."

"AS STEPS ARE TAKEN TO BETTER PREPARE CHILDREN FOR SCHOOLS, WE MUST ALSO BETTER PREPARE SCHOOLS FOR CHILDREN. THIS IS ESPECIALLY IMPORTANT FOR YOUNG CHILDREN. SCHOOLS MUST BE ABLE TO EDUCATE CHILDREN EFFECTIVELY WHEN THEY ARRIVE AT THE SCHOOLHOUSE DOOR, REGARDLESS OF VARIATIONS IN STUDENTS' INTERESTS, CAPACITIES, OR LEARNING STYLES."

—AMERICA 2000, AN EDUCATION STRATEGY

SUGGESTIONS FOR SUCCESSFUL MULTIAGE CLASSROOMS

- Provide plenty of flexible space and divide it into functional areas or "learning centers."
- Supply a selection of concrete materials to foster math concepts and language play. You won't need multiple sets of everything, since most activities will only involve a few children at a time.
- Provide a variety of "real books" (magazines, newspapers, and storybooks) at every reading level. If you do use reading textbooks, do so only as a check. Students in a nongraded class also have different reading levels, so have a variety of reading materials available.
- Structure opportunities for older children to tutor younger ones into the day. Pair a child at the early edge of acquiring a skill with one who is more confident but still needs practice. Or, allow an older student to check a younger one's work.
- Involve students in making work plans or "contracts" on a daily, weekly, or monthly basis.
- Allow children to explore the room freely and to choose their activities individually or in groups.
- Structure the curriculum around themes that integrate learning across content areas.
- Use plenty of support staff—in art, music, physical education,and special needs. Be sure to include this staff in planning curriculum themes.
- Don't sort, track, label, or retain kids. Break down the idea that June is "promotion" time. Students can remain in a group until their mastery of appropriate skills shows they are ready to move on.
- Try sharing responsibilities with another teacher if your subject-matter expertise lies in different areas.
- Switch teaching assignments frequently in graded schools. This increases empathy and cooperation among teachers, familiarizes them with students of different ages, and helps them think of themselves as learners.
- Train student teachers in many grades, not just one. Include courses in early childhood development in their requirements for certification.

Source: *American Educator*, Summer 1990, American Federation of Teachers.

INFORMED AND EDUCATED TEACHERS AND PARENTS.

Research has found that understanding and support of the nongraded program by teachers and parents are the factors most crucial to the program's success.

One of the first steps for teachers is to become knowledgeable about nongraded education by reading professional literature and coming to understand the theoretical aspect of it, believes Bredecamp of the NAEYC. The next piece is to understand the practical side.

Teachers need opportunities to have interaction with people who also are heading toward the nongraded primary. This interaction could be through professional conferences where they share ideas and get involved with colleagues working in nongraded primaries. Then, they will be ready to examine their own classroom environment—how this approach can be used to support developmentally appropriate education for young children.

"Our goal is to have all children learning and all children succeeding and make schools user-friendly for the children," says Bredecamp. "We have to look at who the client is— what children are like developmentally; what their needs are—not just academically and intellectually, but physically, socially, and emotionally. Every child in America should love school, not just a few. It must be exciting and challenging for all children."

Winning parent support. Perhaps the greatest challenge in moving to the nongraded school is explaining its benefits to parents. Virtually all parents want the best for their children, yet many may not have studied how children learn.

A TEACHER'S PERSPECTIVE

"I think administratively a school district has to have its information well in hand before the district can expect teachers to flow into it," says multiage teacher Marsha McCoy of Stark Elementary School in Texas.

"If the teachers are not interested and curious about the program and believe it will take off, I don't think it's for them. You have to go slow and sure. My principal was behind me 150 percent. Anything that happened— he was going to back me up. He was very supportive as our school moved into the program.

"Some teachers can't jump right into it. It's not for everybody. We are very much like a family. It's a lot like the one-room classroom of olden days.

"For grading I use portfolios," she says. "Again, this is difficult for some teachers who are used to a traditional grade book. It's hard for them to leave something like that.

"My students' portfolios include projects chosen by the students. We sit down and go over their work. I also have an assessment form similar to a report card that goes home three times with the portfolios. It's called a self-evaluation card. Inside we ask parents to sit with their child and review the material. They have to evaluate their progress. For example, if the child's penmanship is poor, the child and parent discuss ways the child can improve on it."

Parents are so enthusiastic about McCoy's nongraded program, they must apply for their students to be in the class. Last year when students left the district, the principal held a lottery among parents to fill the vacancies.

"I have had parents speak for the program," McCoy says. "That was my best sales pitch. I was on a speaking panel and called my parents to come to the school where I was speaking and be a part of the audience. They stood up and told how their children had gained. It was tremendous. I was just beaming. Now I have parents who go out and speak on behalf of the program.

"I really feel that motivation in a classroom like this comes from the teacher's enthusiasm. The students are going to model the attitude they see in their teachers. The students, in turn, gain self-motivation. The enthusiasm goes right back into the students."

Parents' first school memories are usually of elementary grades. Many remember structured lessons and rigid routines. They naturally assume that such practices are necessary for learning. Building a bridge of understanding about the nongraded primary between parents and the school staff, with mutual trust and respect, is crucial for the success of the nongraded program.

Schools may start by assessing the role of parents in the nongraded program. How will communications take place between teachers and parents? What is the school climate? Are parents encouraged to visit the school? Do they feel welcome when they do? Do parents feel they have any significant decision-making role? Is the school sensitive to demands in the lives of families?

TEACHING STRATEGIES FOR MIXED-AGE GROUPING

The Case for Mixed-Age Grouping, by Lilian G. Katz, Demetra Evangelou, and Jeanette Allison Hartman, notes, "Teaching strategies appropriate for mixed-age groups are the same as for any early childhood setting." However, some strategies deserve special emphasis:

1. **Promoting social development.** In a mixed-age class, teachers may have to intervene deliberately to stimulate cross-age interaction, especially at first. The teacher should:
    - ⊃ Suggest that older children assist younger ones and that younger ones request assistance from older ones in social situations.
    - ⊃ Encourage older children to assume responsibility for younger ones, and encourage younger ones to rely on older ones.
    - ⊃ Guard against younger children becoming burdens or nuisances for older ones.
    - ⊃ Help children accept their present limitations.
    - ⊃ Help children develop appreciation of their own earlier efforts and progress.
    - ⊃ Discourage stereotyping by age.

2. **Enhancing emotional development.** Evidence shows children respond to the feelings and moods of those around them very early in life. Teachers can channel this responsiveness in two ways:
    - ⊃ Alert children to their peers' need, feelings, and desires.
    - ⊃ Encourage children to give and to accept comfort from each other at times of special stress or anxiety.

3. **Encouraging intellectual development.** When the curriculum encourages children to work together on a variety of tasks, projects, and other activities, the teacher can use cross-age interaction for several intellectual and cognitive benefits:
    - ⊃ Alert children to their peers' interests. For example, the teacher might ask one child to respond to what another has said simply by asking, "What do you think about that, Annie?"
    - ⊃ Alert children to their peers' skills, as appropriate.
    - ⊃ Encourage children to read to others and to listen to others read.
    - ⊃ Help older children think through appropriate roles for younger ones.

Source: National Association for the Education of Young Children, Washington, D.C.

ESTABLISHING A NONGRADED PRIMARY

DEVELOPING AN EDUCATIONAL PHILOSOPHY

An educational philosophy will serve as the basis for planning and implementing a nongraded primary program. This philosophy should reflect the school's beliefs, values, and priorities.

The following questions and points are modified from the *Tennessee Plan for Nongraded Elementary Education* and are meant to stimulate group discussions:

1. What do you believe about how children learn? Primary students are active learners. They need hands-on exploration and freedom to move and interact with peers and adults in conversation and shared tasks and a balance of "work" and "play." Young children learn from each other; they vary widely in level and rate of development in different areas.

2. What do you believe about motivation and what prompts children to learn? Elementary children have inborn motivation to understand their world, to have an effect on it, and to function competently in it. This motivation varies with individuals and changes in form over time. Children respond positively to outside rewards also. What rewards are important: praise, recognition, personal satisfaction, material, or symbolic compensation? What role do sanctions play and why?

3. What do you believe children need to learn? Children need a rich, varied environment of objects, situations, people, backgrounds, experiences, and skills with which to interact. What is the role of the school in each of these areas?

4. Who do you believe has the responsibility and right to be involved in the development and education of young children? Parents have a legal and moral responsibility for their children's welfare and development. Schools have a legal and moral responsibility to provide an educational environment to all children. What are the rights and responsibilities of different adults: parents, community members, teachers, and principals?

5. What do you believe is important about the nature and events within the social, physical, and time environment? Elementary students need to be able to move and to interact with the environment and with others. How should time be distributed and used? What are the space limits of the learning environment (classroom, playground, outdoor classroom, parks, businesses, community services)? How will opportunities for students to interact be provided? (*The Wonder Years*, Kentucky Department of Education).

DIFFERENT WAYS TO GROUP CHILDREN
OF DIFFERENT AGES

One key to the success of a multiage classroom is a variety of groupings that afford students the chance to advance at their own rate, tutor others, and mix with different children. Some types of grouping are:

- **Problem-solving grouping.** Learners are grouped around a common unsolved topic or problem, such as a group discussion related to the main idea of a story.
- **Needs-requirement grouping.** Students are instructed in a concept, skill, or value, such as extra instruction in consonant blends.
- **Reinforcement grouping.** Learners who need more work in a specific area or task are grouped together.
- **Interest grouping.** Learners who are working on a common activity, such as reading poetry aloud, work together.
- **Learning-style grouping.** Children with a common pattern of learning—for example, through manipulation of objects—work with each other.

Source: *Language Arts Handbook for Primary-Grade Teachers in Multi-Graded Classrooms.* Winnipeg, Canada: Manitoba Department of Education, 1988 (in *American Educator*).

ORGANIZING THE TRANSITION

As mentioned earlier, organizing a nongraded primary program requires everyone involved in the process—teachers, administrators, parents—to plan together and consider carefully their needs, the children's needs, and the needs of the whole school community. The following suggestions are from materials developed by the Kentucky Department of Education:

1. **Exploration.** This might be called the awareness stage. The district must help the entire school community understand the primary school concept. Change is gradual and continuous, and occurs only with understanding, acceptance, and support.

Engage staff in lively discussions so that everyone will have an opportunity to be tuned in. Include parents in this orientation. This is a time for exploration: sharing and discussing questions: Why do we need to change? Who is teaching this way and how is it going? Identify resources—people, materials, schools—that can provide information and guidance.

Develop a position statement, critical attributes, and resolve key issues. Create a vision and a process to shift from a skills-based program. Undertake changes necessary to transform early elementary education to achieve the vision. Develop group consensus in a written philosophy statement to serve as the school's guide in planning and implementation. It should reflect the schools beliefs, values, and priorities (See page 16).

2. **Orientation.** Primary, intermediate, and special teachers, as well as librarians, school counselors, and support staff, should be involved in all stages of this process, along with parents.

This stage is the time to build ownership and get ready for the change. It involves the development of individual and building-level philosophy (What do I believe about how children learn? What does the district believe?), self-study (Where am I as a teacher?, What am I already doing that will work well in a nongraded primary? What competencies, knowledge, and skills do I need to develop?), and building-level planning (Where are we as a staff? What curriculum changes are needed?).

Apply information learned from the exploration stage to district, school, and individual considerations of curriculum and instruction, organization, assessment, and the learning environment for primary school. District decision-makers, such as superintendents and board members, should be involved in the process.

Provide opportunities for extensive staff development. Teachers need to learn how to become collaborators/ partners and study alternate ways for student grouping and pupil movement. Teachers need to be involved in the development and implementation of the nongraded model that will be used.

The principal might organize the school into task forces responsible for functions such as scheduling visits to resource schools, developing plans for the home/school partnership, and revitalizing teaching and learning issues (the teacher as facilitator and the child as an active, enthusiastic explorer).

Develop an action plan that will put in place a systematic process to develop a curriculum, instructional method, and a learning environment that will enable students to move to the nongraded primary school experience.

3. Implementation. Implement the action plan. This is a process, not an event. Plans must reflect continuous progress, over time. Go slowly and help teachers take steps as they are ready. Diversity among teachers, as well as among children, must be acknowledged and accepted. Start at a level where teachers are currently working and help them grow from there.

Keep parents and the community informed and aware of the nongraded program through such activities as open houses, PTA meetings, stories in local newspapers, a speakers bureau, public affairs programs, and letters to the home. During the year, sponsor success and celebration activities, not only in the school, but in the community.

Evaluate the action plan throughout the year and make adjustments as needed.

CHARACTERISTICS OF YOUNG LEARNERS

⊃ Young children are innately curious and will strive to learn.
⊃ Playful activity is a natural way of learning.
⊃ Young children learn by imitating, talking, and interacting with each other, as well as with adults.
⊃ Concrete and multisensory materials are children's tools for learning.
⊃ Young children can simultaneously acquire knowledge and skills in many areas.
⊃ Learning occurs at different rates.
⊃ Real-life experiences related to the interests of children promote learning.
⊃ Learning impacts the "whole" child, and vice versa.
⊃ Experiencing successes builds a sense of security and self-confidence.

Source: *Program Advisory*, May 1991, Kentucky Department of Education.

A NONGRADED PRIMARY IN ACTION

In 1990, the Kentucky legislature approved a sweeping school reform package that included a statewide preschool program and the elimination of all grade levels below fourth grade. The program is called "Primary School," rather than "Nongraded Primary School," because the definition and tenets required by the state's education reform act are broader than the concept of "nongradedness." The primary school in Kentucky is nongraded, but it is many other things as well.

In 1991, Jackson Elementary School in Fort Campbell, Kentucky, launched the School of Choice: Graded and Nongraded Program. It features team teaching, developmental placement, and multiage grouping (students are placed in "families" with a three-year age span, allowing for a wide range of developmental interests and abilities). The graded program features a variety of teaching methods and a teacher adviser system.

Both programs emphasize active learning and enrichment activities, says Principal Donald E. Rush. He says the program also focuses on the skills essential for living successfully in an ever-more complex world.

Located on a military base, Jackson is part of the Fort Campbell Schools and enrolls 906 prekindergarten through fifth-grade children who live on the base. Rush says the new program spent approximately $20,000 on in-service training alone, including visits to other schools and programs.

Rush says his interest in nongraded education goes back about 30 years. In moving to the new program, he says, the school suffered all of the expected adjustment problems, "It was frustrating until about January when people started to get a handle on it and said, 'Hey, I can do this.'" Now, he says, many teachers who are in the graded program look forward to becoming involved in the nongraded program.

In the beginning, Rush explains, teachers were given a choice of whether to opt for the graded or the nongraded program. In preparation for the change, teachers were given an opportunity to visit programs in other school districts. "It was absolutely essential that we visit other schools," Rush says. "We took a series of questions about how a program should be implemented. The visits changed the mindset of some teachers. After that we spent a year discussing what it would be like in our school. Today, I would say that's not long enough. We followed what we thought would be the ideal and it still caused us some stress."

(continued on the next page)

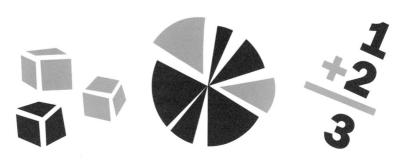

(continued from previous page)

In working with parents, Jackson Elementary School held special meetings about the new program in the spring and followed up with an orientation for parents in the fall. "I thought we had fully explained the program and that was enough," he adds, "but I was wrong."

In January a group of parents announced its intentions to go around the school and superintendent to the school board to stop the approach. Fortunately, Rush says, "We had just completed a survey of parents and the feedback was positive and drew support for the program."

Jackson Elementary School teacher Faye Garnett supports Rush's views. "The program works extremely well," she says. "We already had multiage grouping. Parents are an integral part of our system and are encouraged to offer their suggestions. When a child needs extra help, we address it as a partnership."

Garnett says that the nongraded program "is not anything for anyone to become apprehensive about. Many of the teachers here have found that they are more effective in the nongraded system. We also have a dynamic staff development program. If teachers read or hear about a new concept, then we try to find out all we can about it to determine if it will effectively help in our new system."

PRIMARY PROGRAM GLOSSARY

Here are some common terms for persons just starting to learn about the nongraded primary program. Many of these terms were adopted by the Kentucky State Department of Education. Individual understanding of these terms may vary.

ANECDOTAL RECORD.

A written record kept in a positive tone of a child's progress based on milestones particular to that child's social, emotional, physical, aesthetic, and cognitive development. Recording happens throughout the day while actual activities are occurring. Recordings are made when appropriate and are not forced, in other words you may go a few days without reporting on a particular child if there is nothing that bears recording.

This method is informal and encourages the use of notes or a checklist with space for comments. Continuous notes are recorded about what a child can do and his or her achievements, as opposed to what he or she cannot do. Instead of writing "John has been a continuous discipline problem. Today he participated in a group for 10 minutes, but then started distracting the other students and had to be removed," the anecdotal record may read something like "John contributed attentively in group time for 10 minutes."

AUTHENTIC ASSESSMENT.

An assessment of what the teacher actually wants students to be able to do or understand. Assessment occurs in the context of normal classroom involvement and reflects the actual learning experience. Portfolios, journals, observations, taped readings, videotapes, and conferences are examples. The tasks are frequently open-ended and judgment is required to evaluate the level of performance.

COLLABORATION.

Planning, involving, and supporting students by two or more concerned groups—teachers, aides, itinerant and resource teachers, parents, and community representatives.

CONTINUOUS PROGRESS.

A student's unique progression through the primary program at his or her own rate without the comparison of others. Retention, promotion, and assigned letter grades are not compatible with this progression. The curriculum and expectations for student performance in a continuous progress program are not linked to the child's age or number of years in school.

COOPERATIVE LEARNING.

An extensively researched instructional method in which students are heterogeneously grouped to produce academic and social gains. Students are individually accountable for their learning, yet also experience a sense of interdependency for the success of their group.

CRITICAL ATTRIBUTES.

Descriptors that define necessary components of the primary program. They are developmentally appropriate educational practices, multiage/multiability classrooms, continuous progress, authentic assessment, qualitative reporting methods, professional teamwork, and positive parent involvement.

CURRICULUM FRAMEWORK.

A statewide guide to influence curriculum development and instructional decision making at the local level. The framework for Kentucky's Primary Program identifies teaching and assessment strategies, instructional material resources, ideas on how to incorporate the resources of the community, a directory of model teaching sites, and alternative ways of using school time.

DEPARTMENTALIZED TEACHING.

Two or more teachers who teach the same children different subjects. For example, Teacher A is responsible for reading, social studies, and art, while Teacher B provides math, science, and writing instruction. The teaching is isolated and does not require any collaboration of planning or implementation. This practice is *not* consistent with the nongraded primary program.

DEVELOPMENTAL APPROPRIATENESS.

This concept has two dimensions:

Age appropriateness: Human development research indicates universal, predictable milestones of growth and change that occur in children during the first nine years of life. These predictable changes occur in all domains of development—physical, emotional, social, cognitive, and aesthetic. Knowledge of the typical development of children within the age span served by an educational program provides a framework for teachers to use when preparing the learning environment and planning appropriate experiences.

Individual appropriateness: Each child is a unique person with an individual pattern and timing of growth, as well as individual personality, learning style, and family background. The curriculum and adults' interactions with children should be responsive to individual differences. Learning in young children is the result of interaction between the child's thoughts and experiences with materials, ideas, and people. When these experiences match the child's developing abilities, and also challenge the child's interest and

understanding, learning will take place. (*The Teacher's Ongoing Role in Creating a Developmentally Appropriate Early Childhood Program*, Connecticut Department of Education).

DEVELOPMENTALLY APPROPRIATE EDUCATIONAL PRACTICES.

Those educational practices and curriculum components that coincide with and foster developmental appropriateness. These would include an integrated curriculum, active child involvement and interaction, use of manipulatives and multisensory activities, a balance of teacher-directed and child-initiated activities, varied instructional strategies, and flexible groupings and regroupings.

DEVELOPMENTALLY APPROPRIATE ENVIRONMENTS.

Settings that coincide with and foster children's developmental growth—tables or grouped desks instead of rows of separated desks, easily accessible shelves with varied materials for a wide range of uses, and a home-like setting.

FAMILY GROUPING.

A group of students who stay with the same classmates and teacher(s) for more than one year. For example, in a multiage grouping of six-, seven-, and eight-year-olds, approximately a third of the class would stay the same, a third would move to fourth grade, and a third would be new to the class. A child could be in this class for three years.

FLEXIBLE GROUPING.

A combination of homogeneous and heterogeneous grouping on an ad hoc basis.

HETEROGENEOUS GROUPING.

The grouping of children based on their differences—age, sex, race, or achievement. A heterogeneous group would be composed of girls and boys of mixed ages and abilities.

HOMOGENEOUS GROUPING.

The grouping of children based on their similarities, such as age, ability, or test scores. For example, John may be in Mrs. Smith's room because he is seven years old, and this is his second year of school. He is in the red reading group because he is a good reader, but receives special tutoring in math because his standardized test score was lower than a particular number. John was homogeneously grouped each time. This practice is *not* consistent with a nongraded primary program.

INTEGRATED CURRICULUM.

Cutting across subject matter lines to bring together various curricular content areas in a meaningful and true-to-life association. Theme study is a technique for integrating curricula, but not all integrated curricula revolve around a theme. Whole language and writing across the curriculum are examples of integrated approaches that may or may not involve a thematic approach.

INTEGRATION/CORRELATION.

Teaching strategies where concepts and skills from several content areas are taught simultaneously with a particular theme, topic, or project. When the natural connections among the various content areas are recognized and teaching is structured to acknowledge and reinforce them, integration or correlation occurs. In integration, there are no content boundaries. When subject areas remain discrete, but a common theme serves as the organizer for developing instruction in each, then correlation is occurring.

LITERATURE-BASED INSTRUCTION.

A strategy for teaching reading using literature as the foundation. The language arts components (spelling and grammar) and content areas are taught around a particular book or piece of literature. From this base, skill development and related activities evolve. Multiple copies of books that represent a wide range of literary categories—fiction, nonfiction-fiction, and poetry—are essential.

MANIPULATIVES.

Concrete or hands-on instructional materials and games used in the classroom to introduce and reinforce skills (especially in math). The use of manipulatives is developmentally appropriate for young children who need to learn by using real objects. Examples include geometric puzzles, building blocks, and measuring cups.

NONGRADED (UNGRADED).

Term used to describe schools, classes, or curricula, without concern for the grades a child is in school, such as first, second, or third grade (not to be confused with the elimination of letter grades).

NONGRADED (UNGRADED) PRIMARY SCHOOL.

A school with a flexible system for grouping children together regardless of age and number of years in school. Extensive efforts are made to adapt instruction to individual differences.

PERFORMANCE ASSESSMENT.

Assessment based on a child's actual performance within the context of the classroom, as opposed to assessment from tests or written assignments that could differ from the processes a child used while learning the material.

POSITIVE PARENT INVOLVEMENT.

The establishment of productive relationships between the school and the home to enhance communication, promote understanding, and provide opportunities for children to interact with people, places, and things in their immediate environment and beyond.

PROFESSIONAL TEAMWORK.

Members of the professional staff have regular opportunities to exchange information and ideas and cooperatively plan the instructional program. They may use team or collaborative teaching and peer coaching to meet the needs of the students and provide support and assistance for each other.

QUALITATIVE REPORTING METHODS.

Regular home-school communications describing how and what the child is learning, individual accomplishments, interests, abilities, and attitudes. Progress is related in terms of the continuous growth and development of the whole child in noncomparative ways. Reporting encompasses formats such as formal narrative report cards, conferences, portfolios, journals, videotapes, and anecdotal records.

TEAM TEACHING.
Two or more teachers who plan, teach, and support each other with common and agreed upon roles and responsibilities. They teach to a combined group of students, which may be grouped and regrouped.

THEMATIC APPROACH TO CURRICULUM.
An approach to learning that motivates students to investigate interesting ideas from multiple perspectives. The central theme becomes the catalyst for developing concepts, generalizations, skills, and attitudes. The rationale is grounded in a philosophy that young children learn most efficiently when they perceive subjects as worthy of their time, attention, and inquiry. These themes may be broad-based or narrow in scope, may be used in designated classes or the whole school, and may last for a few weeks to several months.

TRACKING.
Designated groupings, which can last through the duration of schooling, reflecting students' abilities or interests. There may be tracks for slow, average, and fast learners. In high school, there may be tracks for college-bound and vocational education students. This practice is *not* consistent with the nongraded primary program.

VALUED OUTCOME.
Ability to complete tasks that have application to "real life" and are valued by the student and the adult world (Council on School Performance Standards).

WHOLE LANGUAGE.
A dynamic, evolving philosophy with the core being the understanding that listening, speaking, writing, and reading are not isolated for study but permeate the whole curriculum. Language is taught as a "whole," not by fragmented skills. Teachers and children take significant responsibility for learning and are involved actively in all the processes (listening, speaking, writing, and reading) at all times.

REFERENCES

Anderson, Robert H. and Goodlad, John I. *The Nongraded Elementary School.* Revised Edition. Teachers College Press, 1987.

Black, Janet K. and Puckett, Margaret B. *Informing Others About Developmentally Appropriate Practice.*

Cohen, Deborah L. "A Look at Multi-Age Classrooms." *Education Digest,* May 1990.

Cushman, Kathleen. *American Educator.* Summer 1990.

Education USA. National School Public Relations Association, Arlington, Va.

Gaustad, Joan. "Making the Transition from Graded to Nongraded Primary Education." *Oregon School Study Council Bulletin,* April 1992.

Kantrowitz, Barbara and Wingert, Pat. "How Kids Learn." *Newsweek,* April 17, 1989.

Katz, Lilian G.; Evangelou, Demetra; and Hartman, Jeanette Allison. *The Case for Mixed-Age Grouping in Early Childhood Education.* National Association for the Education of Young Children, Washington, D.C.

Lodish, Richard. *The Pros and Cons of Mixed-Age Grouping.* Alexandria, Va.: National Association of Elementary School Principals, 1992.

NAEYC Position Statement on Developmentally Appropriate Practice in the Primary Grades Serving 5- Through 8-Year-Olds. The National Association for the Education of Young Children, Washington, D.C.

"Nongraded Education." *ERS Bulletin,* June 1992.

Project Real School, Executive Summary. San Diego City Schools, Calif.

"Profiles in Excellence." *The Executive Educator,* February 1992, National School Boards Association.

Smith, Lee I. *Teaching in a Nongraded School.* West Nyack, N.Y.: Parker Publishing Co., 1971.

The Wonder Years. Kentucky Department of Education, Frankfort, Ky.

Webb, Tamsen Banks. *Multi-Age Grouping in the Early Years: Building Upon Children's Developmental Strengths.*

ACKNOWLEDGMENTS

The Nongraded Primary...Making Schools Fit Children is a publication of the American Association of School Administrators, 1801 North Moore Street, Arlington, Virginia 22209-9988. The need for concise, current information on the nongraded primary was the driving force behind this booklet.

Author Rodney Davis has been involved in education for over 22 years. Currently, he is director of information services for the Dallas Independent School District, where he also taught high school, and senior editor of *Better Teaching*, the newsletter of the Parent Institute in Fairfax, Virginia. Davis is also publisher of the *Texas Superintendents' Insider*.

Special thanks to David Hornbeck of the Kentucky Department of Eduction and to Dr. Ernest Boyer for taking time to contribute their insights and comments. The author also expresses his appreciation to Bob Hockstein, Vicki Phillips, Rosie Sorrells, Nancy Barker, Phil George, Margaret Peterson, and the other educators cited in this publication.

Gary Marx, senior associate executive director, served as project manager. Leslie Eckard, associate editor, edited the manuscript and provided direction, with editorial and production assistance from Katie Ross, communications assistant. Graphic design was provided by Lea Croteau of East Woods Studio.